ROCKS, MINERALS, AND RESOURCES

Sand and Soil
Earth's building blocks

Beth Gurney

Crabtree Publishing Company
www.crabtreebooks.com

Crabtree Publishing Company

www.crabtreebooks.com

Coordinating editor: Ellen Rodger

Production coordinator: Rosie Gowsell

Project editor: Carrie Gleason

Proofreader and Indexer: Adrianna Morganelli

Art director: Rob MacGregor

Design: Rosie Gowsell, Samara Parent

Production assistant: Samara Parent

Photo research: Allison Napier

Consultant: Dr. Richard Cheel, Professor of Earth Sciences, Brock University

Photographs: Paul Almasy/CORBIS: p. 22; Botanica/Getty Images: p. 23 (Top right); Dr. Jeremy Bergess/ Science Photo Library: p. 12 (bottom left), p. 13 (bottom); Scott Camazine/ Photo Researchers, Inc: p. 14 (top right); Clouds Hill Imaging Ltd./ CORBIS: p. 13 (top right); Dean Conger/ CORBIS: p. 26; Kevin Fleming/ CORBIS: p. 29; Michael P. Gadomski/ Photo Researchers, Inc: p. 30; Roger De La Harpe, Gallo Images/ CORBIS: p. 17; Ted Horowitz/ CORBIS: p.9 (bottom right); Earl and Nazima Kowall/ CORBIS: p. 27 (top right); Gideon Mendel/ CORBIS: p. 1; Hank Morgan/ Photo Researchers, Inc: p. 18; North Wind/ North Wind Pictures: p. 20; Gianni Dagli Orti/ CORBIS: p.21 (top right); Samara Parent: p. 15 (top left); Dr. David Patterson/ Science Photo Library: p. 12 (top right); PICIMPACT/CORBIS: p. 10; Lynda Richardson/ CORBIS: p. 27

(bottom); Joel W. Rogers/ CORBIS: p. 28; Rosenfeld Images Ltd./ Photo Researchers, Inc: p. 9 (top left); Scott T. Smith/ CORBIS: p. 25 (top left); Stone/ Getty Images: p. 15 (bottom right), p. 21 (bottom); Jim Sugar/ CORBIS: p. 24; Taxi/ Getty Images: p.22 (bottom left); Sheila Terry/ Science Photo Library: p. 25 (bottom right); Sven Torfinn/ Panos Pictures: p. 31; Ron Watts/ CORBIS: p. 8; Stuart Westmorland/ CORBIS: p. 23 (bottom left)

Illustrations: Connie Gleason: contents page; Dan Pressman: p. 6, p. 11, p. 17; David Wysotski, Allure Illustrations: pp. 4-5

Map: Jim Chernishenko: p. 19

Cover: Deserts are arid regions where sand dunes support very little plant life.

Title page: A farmer in Africa plants peanuts in freshly turned soil.

Crabtree Publishing Company

www.crabtreebooks.com   1-800-387-7650

Cataloging-in-Publication Data

Gurney, Beth.
  Sand and soil / written by Beth Gurney.
    p. cm. -- (Rocks, minerals, and resources)
  Includes index.
  ISBN 0-7787-1417-9 (rlb) -- ISBN 0-7787-1449-7 (pbk)
  1. Soils--Juvenile literature. 2. Sand--Juvenile literature.
I. Title. II. Series.
    S591.3.G87 2005
    631.4--dc22
                                    2004012810
                                    LC

Published in the United States
PMB 16A
350 Fifth Ave.
Suite 3308
New York, NY
10118

Published in Canada
616 Welland Ave.,
St. Catharines,
Ontario, Canada
L2M 5V6

Published in the United Kingdom
73 Lime Walk
Headington
Oxford
0X3 7AD
United Kingdom

Published in Australia
386 Mt. Alexander Rd.,
Ascot Vale (Melbourne)
V1C 3032

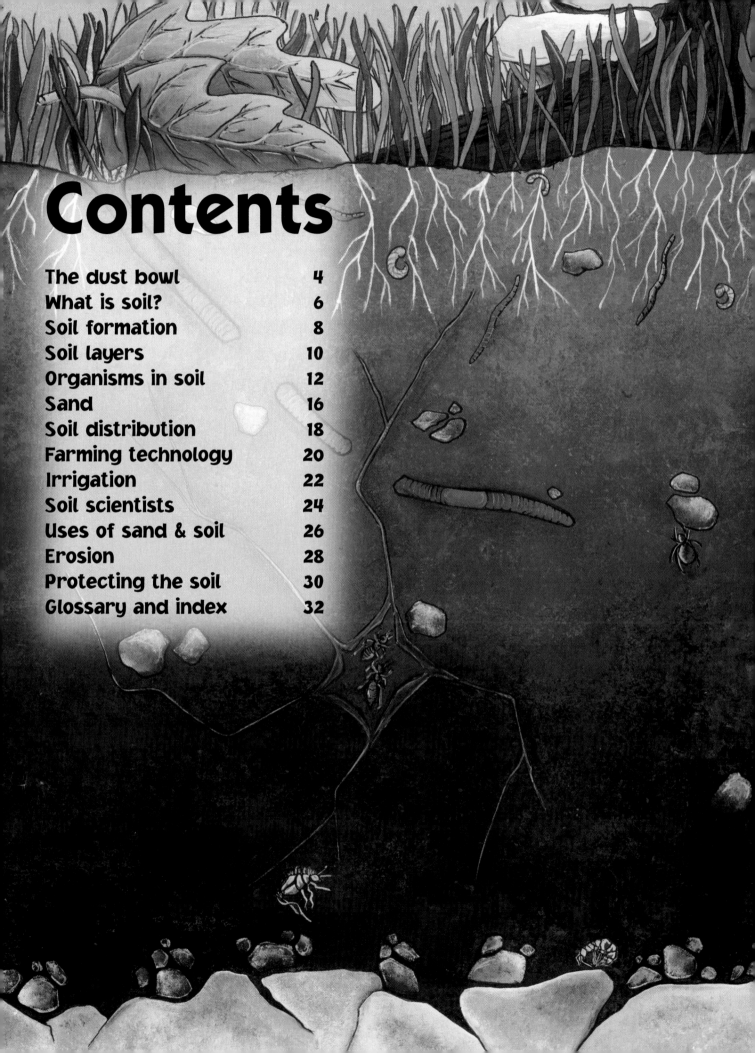

Contents

The dust bowl

The farmer raised his hand to shelter his eyes from the swirling debris as a great gust of wind whipped across the farm. As the wind blew, valuable topsoil was lifted from the parched open fields. Several years of little rain made the soil light and dry. The gales swept the brown soil up into the sky, forming a black blizzard. The dark cloud of wind carried the soil eastward, covering homes and cars thousands of miles away in dirt. Without the rich topsoil, the farmer's land could no longer produce crops. With no crops to sell, many farmers lost their livelihoods. This period in history has been given the name "The Dirty Thirties."

Life-giving soil

When European settlers first came to North America in the 1600s, **fertile** land was plentiful. No one ever considered the need to preserve and protect the soil. Eventually, settlers moved westward and farmers cut down the trees and grass to make new farmland. The soil was left without plants to protect it from the rain, snow, and wind. By the 1930s, over-farming had damaged the once fertile soil. Since this time, farmers have learned ways to conserve and protect their valuable soil.

Soil is essential for all life on earth because it provides a place for crops and plants to grow. Without soil, forests and jungles would not exist. Soil also relies on the plants, too. Plants keep soil in place and supply it with **nutrients**.

What is soil?

Soil is the thin layer on the surface of the earth made up of rocks, water, air, and living organisms. It contains many organic and inorganic elements that, when they work together, provide nutrients for plants.

Rock particles

Rock particles are inorganic material, which means they are not living organisms. Rock particles make up more than half of soil. Rock particles come from larger rocks, called the parent rock. The parent rock determines what the soil will look like, what it will feel like, and what kind of plant life it can support. Different rocks contain different **minerals**, depending on how they are formed. Different plants need different minerals to live.

Water in soil

Water is needed for soil to sustain plant life. When it rains, or when plants are **irrigated**, water **leaches** underground. It travels through pores, or air pockets, in the soil. Plants feed off the water by absorbing it through their roots.

Weathering

Rock particles are broken down from parent rock in a process called weathering.

1. Wind-blown sand rubs away at rock.
2. Glaciers carry bigger rocks that scrape the rocks underneath.
3. Freezing water expands in cracks and pushes rocks apart.
4. Plant and tree roots wedge between rocks and push them apart.
5. All of these factors make the rock particles break off from the parent rock.
6. Rock particles mix with organic material to form soil.

Air in soil

Air is also an important part of soil. Within the soil, pockets of air are trapped. These pockets provide a place for water to be stored, and also provide oxygen so that animals that dwell in the soil, such as earthworms, moles, and mites, can breathe underground.

Soil nutrients

Organic matter helps provide nutrients to soil. The word organic refers to living things, such as plants and animals. When plants and animals die, their bodies decay, or are broken down. Leaves that fall from trees in autumn are scattered on the ground. The leaves eventually begin to break down because of the weather and the organisms that feed on the leaves. As leaves break down, any nutrients stored in them are taken in by the soil. The plants and animals that live in the soil take in these nutrients.

Balancing act

Healthy soil must have a balance of inorganic material, water, air, and organic material. Soil that is too **compact** does not have air pockets. This may cause flooding because water is unable to leach, or dissolve, into the ground.

Humus is dead organic matter. Leaves from trees fall on the forest floor, and are broken down by the weather and bacteria. The nutrients in the leaves enrich the soil.

The many animals that live in the soil and help keep it healthy do not survive in compact soil, as there is not enough oxygen. Soil without organic material does not have the nutrients that plant life needs.

Soil formation

Soil takes hundreds of years to form. It has a very long life cycle. It can take about 500 years for one inch (2.5 cm) of soil to form. By digging underground to look at the soil, people can learn about what the climate has been like in that area for many years.

Soil cycle

The soil cycle begins with rock. Forces such as wind, rain, and temperature have an impact on rock. Wind and water cause rock to break down over time, and changes in temperature cause rock to **expand** and **contract**, creating cracks.

Plants work to create the beginnings of new soil. **Lichen** is often the first plant to form on bare rock. Lichen roots itself into rock cracks and crevices. As the roots expand and grow, they cause the rock to break down. This mixing of organic plant with inorganic rock is the birth of new soil.

Aging soil

The more plant life that grows on rocks, the more the roots work away to break the rock down. As the plants die, they become the organic matter needed to make healthy soil. Their nutrients are broken down and used to feed new plant life and animals in the soil. The soil grows deeper as the cycle continues. As soil ages, it becomes more balanced. Nutrients that are taken out to support animals and plant life are returned to the soil as other plants and animals die.

Lichen comes in all different colors. The lichen growing on this bare rock is in the Canadian Rockies.

Mature soil is ideal for growing crops, such as these wheat seedlings.

Death of the soil

Sometimes soil's life cycle comes to an abrupt end. Soil that has taken hundreds of years to form can be washed away in an instant by floodwaters. Other natural occurrences, such as volcanic eruptions, cause soil to be covered over and buried. When a covering, such as lava, hardens, it cuts off access to the soil. Sometimes soil is lost because people do not protect it from **erosion**, or they construct buildings on top of fertile soil.

Rebirth

When a volcano erupts, it pours out molten lava, or hot liquid rock. Lava hardens as it cools, forming a rocky surface. The first plants to form on this new rock burrow their roots into the crevices, breaking down some of the rock. This interaction between organic material and rock particles marks the beginnings of new soil.

A new plant begins to grow in a field of hardened lava.

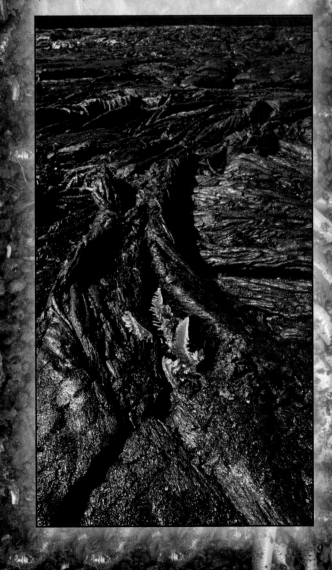

Soil layers

Soil exists in layers called horizons. Soil that is younger, or newer, does not have many layers. Older soils have many different layers. Each one tells the story about the climate and conditions that existed when the soil layer was formed.

Types of soil

Soil types are classified according to the size of particles the soil contains. The size of particles determines how much water can drain through the soil, and how many nutrients are in the soil. Sand has the largest particles in soil. Sand cannot hold nutrients because it does not have any organic material. Silt particles are smaller than sand. Silt is smooth and powdery. Clay particles are the smallest. Soils with a lot of clay have more nutrients, but do not allow much air and water to pass through. How much of each of these particles is in the soil is reflected by the color of the soil. Sandier soils are lighter in color. The more clay present in a soil sample, the darker the soil appears.

Peat is partially decomposed plant matter that is rich in nutrients. Some soils are rich in peat.

Soil variety

Soil horizons come in all different shapes and sizes. Soils are slightly different depending on where in the world they exist, and how they were formed. Sometimes a horizon of soil has very little organic matter, but a great deal of silt or clay. These soil horizons are called fragipans or claypans. Fragipans are very dense. They do not have much air in them, and water cannot easily leach through. They are so hard that plant roots have difficulty penetrating them.

O horizon

The top layer of soil, or horizon, is the O horizon. The O horizon is made up of organic material such as dead leaves. The organic material breaks down and provides nutrients for the plants and animals that feed off the soil.

A horizon

Below the O horizon is the A horizon. The A horizon is home to much of the soil's organic material. This is where many organisms live. Rainwater leaches into the A horizon to provide water for plant roots. This horizon of soil supports the roots of plants and trees.

B horizon

The B horizon is located beneath the A horizon. This layer is home to decomposed organic material and minerals, as well as larger soil particles.

C horizon

The C horizon has less organic material than the A and B layers above it.

R horizon

The C horizon eventually meets the R horizon. The R horizon is made up of bedrock, which is a solid layer of rock that lies beneath the soil.

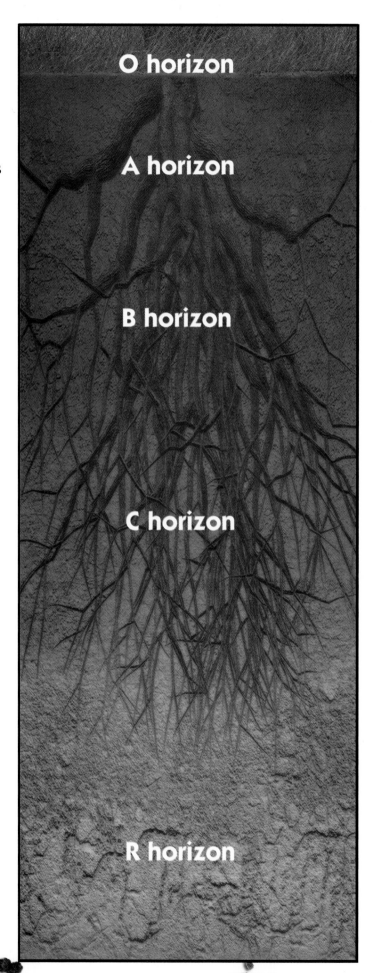

Organisms in soil

Soil is full of different forms of life. The many animals that live in soil are essential to its fertility. Some animals, such as beetles, can be seen. Many organisms, such as bacteria, are so tiny that they cannot be viewed with the naked eye. While they are too tiny to be seen, they play an important role in how soil works to decompose organic matter, and distribute life-giving nutrients, air, and water.

Protozoa

Protozoa are **single-celled** animals. These organisms, such as amoebae and flagellates, can only be seen with a microscope, but they are an important part of the **food web** in soil. They feed on fungi, bacteria, and even other protozoa and release nutrients that plants can use.

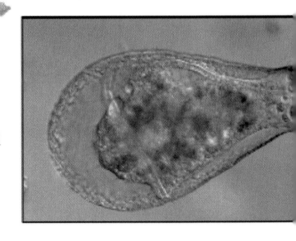

Bacteria

Bacteria cannot be seen by the naked eye but they play a large role in soil health. These single-celled organisms are the foundation of all plant and soil life. There are many different kinds of bacteria in the soil. Their job is to take energy from humus, or nutrient rich decayed plant matter, and use it to feed plants. Plants need bacteria to grow. One teaspoon of topsoil contains about 50 million bacteria. Some bacteria, called **nitrogen**-fixing bacteria, help plants breathe. Plants need nitrogen to survive, but cannot absorb it from the air. Nitrogen-fixing bacteria take in nitrogen gas from the air, and change it into a form that plants can use.

(above) A close-up of a soil amoeba.

(left) A type of bacteria that grows in soil.

Nematodes

Nematodes, sometimes called round worms, are tiny worms. There are thousands of nematodes in each teaspoon of soil. These **parasites** search out bacteria in the soil and eat it. They also live off dead organic matter, and even prey on other round worms. Some types of fungus capture these worms and eat them.

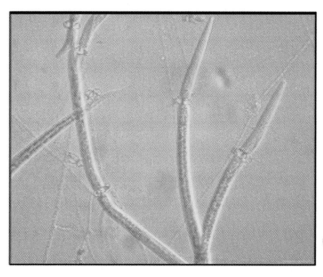

A close-up of a fungus capturing nematodes.

Fungi

Hair-like strands surround many plant roots, but these are not extensions of the roots. These fine threads are a type of fungus called hyphae. The hyphae feed off plant roots, and create intricate networks that stretch for many yards. In some cases, the hyphal network allows different plants to share resources.

A flower that needs sunlight to live may thrive in a shady area by borrowing nutrients from other plants, which are transported through the hyphal network.

(below) The hyphae of the fungi growing off these tree roots are white.

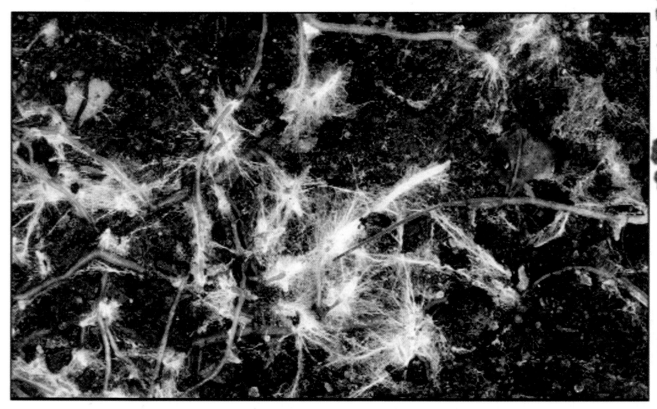

13

Insects

Mites, beetles, millipedes, and other insects and spiders digest the organic matter in soil, and help break it down. Their movement also helps create small pathways so air and water can get into the soil. They also feed on bacteria, protozoa, and fungi. Beetle mites belong to the spider family. They are one of many types of mites that live in the soil. The mites do not work alone. Thousands of mites work through the soil seeking fungus to eat. The mites create pellets from the fungus, which are eaten by bacteria. Bacteria create nutrients that are used by the plants.

Millipedes help create new soil by moving through it.

Prairie dogs dig burrows, or underground nests, in the soil. Their digging helps new soil to form.

Rodents

Prairie dogs, moles, and groundhogs all make their homes underground. They are some of the largest animals that interact with the soil every day. These underground dwellers do not damage the soil. In fact, their digging and burrowing helps to create air pockets in the soil, which soil dwelling animals need to survive. Many of them, such as moles, find their favorite foods, such as earthworms, underground.

Nutrients

People need nutrients to survive. We get these nutrients from the food we eat. Plants also need many nutrients to grow and thrive. Nitrogen, phosphorus, and potassium are three very important nutrients for plants. Without nitrogen, plants that should be green and healthy appear yellow. Phosphorus is used to help plants convert energy from the sun, in a process called **photosynthesis**. Potassium has the job of keeping plants hearty and healthy. It helps keep plant roots in place, and helps plants stay strong even when the weather is too hot, too cold, or there is not enough water. As plants grow, they take up nutrients from the soil. If too many nutrients have been taken out of the soil, they can be replaced artificially by using **fertilizer**.

A woman applies fertlizer to rice plants. Fertilizers are substances that contain nutrients for plants.

Earthworms

Earthworms are one of the most important animals that live in soil. As worms burrow underground they ingest soil, or pass it through their bodies. The soil passes out of the worm, along with the worm's **castings**. This helps break down the soil, and the castings are very rich in nutrients. The presence of earthworms is a sign of healthy soil.

Sand

All soil contains sand particles. Sand is made up of particles that are smaller than gravel, but larger than soil. Unlike soil, sand does not contain any organic material. Most plants cannot grow in sand.

Sand formation

Sand particles come from a variety of sources. They are formed from eroded rock, lava, broken down coral and seashells, or mineral crystals. The color and shape of sand particles depends on the type of rock that it comes from. The whitest sand, like that seen on many tropical beaches, is created from crushed coral. Over time, the waves break the coral down into grains that wash up on the beach.

On the move

Sand does not contain organic material to weigh it down or trap water, so wind and rain move it around easily. Sand is also transported by ice. When water containing sand particles freezes, the sand is trapped in the ice. When the ice moves into a warmer environment and melts, the sand is released.

Only a few plants, such as cacti, grow in sand.

Deserts

Areas that receive less than 10 inches (25 cm) of precipitation each year are called deserts. Deserts in the world's hottest regions look like oceans of sand. About one-third of the Earth's land surface is desert. The world's largest desert is the Sahara. It covers about 3.5 million square miles (91 million square kilometers) in the northern part of Africa. Sand dunes in the Sahara are some of the world's largest.

Some people of the world live in deserts. The San of the Kalahari desert in southern Africa traditionally gather plants and hunt animals.

Sand dunes

When the wind blows on sand it creates dunes. Dunes come in different shapes, depending on how strong the wind is, and the direction it is blowing. Large sand dunes move over time by shifting with the wind.

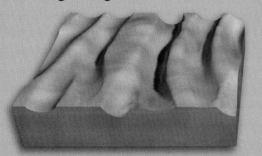

Seif dunes are formed in long ridges.

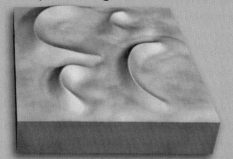

Barchan dunes are crescent shaped dunes. The dunes form a cup shape around large obstacles like boulders.

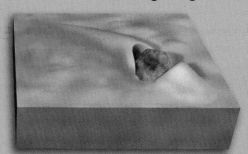

Tail dunes form around obstacles. As the wind travels past these objects it drops the sand particles it is carrying.

Star dunes get their shape from winds blowing from more than one direction, creating the star shape.

Soil distribution

Different regions in the world are home to different types of soil. A region's climate, rock types, and plant life determine what type of soil it will produce. In some warm areas the layer of topsoil will be as deep as sixteen feet (five meters). In colder regions the topsoil layer may be as shallow as half an inch (one centimeter) or less.

Tropical soil

Tropical climates exist in places that lie near the equator. They are usually very hot, get a lot of rainfall, and are able to grow lush plants. Soil forms at a rapid rate in tropical climates, but the soil is not always fertile. The nutrients are often carried deep into the soil by rain before the plants can use them.

Desert soil

Arid or desert regions, such as Arizona, are very hot with little rainfall. They are often home to sandy regions, and their soils do not contain much organic matter.

Temperate soil

In temperate regions soil is not as deep as it is in the tropics. This is because soil production does not usually happen during the cold winter months. The soil often contains more organic matter in these climates because the organic matter does not break down as quickly in colder climates as in the tropics.

In some temperate regions, people grow crops in greenhouses in the winter. Greenhouses are enclosed spaces that trap heat.

Arctic soil

On the Arctic tundra, soil production is even slower than it is in areas with a more temperate, or moderate climate. This is mostly because beneath the soil's surface layer is a layer of soil called permafrost that is always frozen. The cold temperature makes it hard for the plant life necessary for soil production to thrive. Lichen thrive in the Arctic and some do not even need soil to live.

Soil through time

Climate changes that took place thousands of years ago still have an impact on our soil today.

During the Ice Age, glaciers acted like plows, spreading across the land and pushing the soil that lay in its path. Much of the richest farm soil in North America got to where it is now due to glaciers. As these giant masses of ice spread across the land they eroded the rock beneath them, breaking it down into soil particles. When the Ice Age ended and the glaciers receded, this soil was deposited, creating an ideal fertile environment for crop farming. In other areas, the glaciers stripped away the topsoil as they traveled through. In these regions the soil today is new or immature soil.

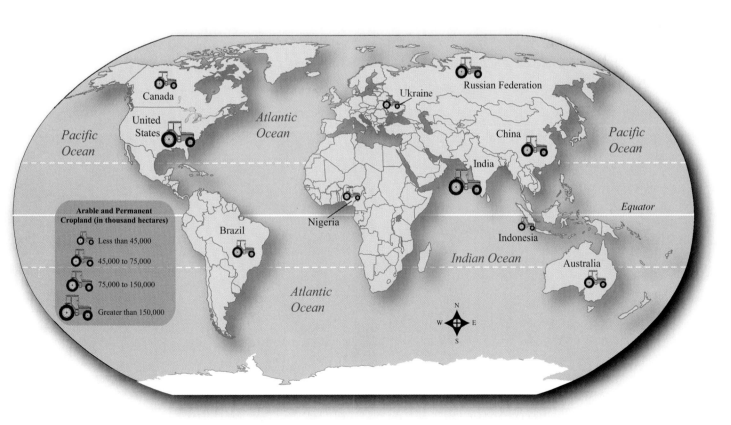

This map shows the top ten countries that have the most arable soil and permanent cropland. Some of the food these countries produce feeds people in regions that do not have good farmland.

Farming technology

Farming played a large role in creating our modern way of living. Thousands of years ago, before farming, people lived nomadic lives, moving from place to place. They followed herds of animals that they hunted for food, and gathered berries, roots, and other plants that grew wild. About 7,000 years ago, in the Middle East, the first farmers began planting seeds from wild grains and harvesting fruits and vegetables.

Early hand tools

Early farmers used a few simple tools, such as sharp sticks to dig holes for planting. In time, a crossbar was added to the stick so farmers could use their foot to drive the tool deeper into the soil. This early instrument resembled the spade, still used today by gardeners. When people began using metal, farming tools were improved. Sharp, strong ends were formed and attached to sticks to make tools that resembled the modern hoe and trowel.

Early plows

The moldboard plow was invented around 300 B.C. in China. A moldboard plow is a cast iron plow with two sloped wings that come together to a point, to cut through the soil. Most Europeans and North Americans used oxen and horses to pull simple wooden plows from the 1500s until the 1700s. In 1814, Thomas Jefferson began making his own moldboard plows, improving on the designs he observed in France. In 1819, Jethro Wood further improved upon the cast iron plow by designing a model that could be broken into three pieces. If one part of the plow was damaged, only the part would have to be replaced instead of the entire plow.

In this illustration, farmers clear the land for farming.

John Deere

John Deere, an American blacksmith, developed the first successful, self-scouring steel plow. Farmers who settled in the North American midwest found that the cast iron plows they used in the sandy soils of the east were not effective in the thick, rich soil of the midwest. Plow blades became caked with earth, and could not turn the soil. John Deere made a sleeker, self-scouring plow from a broken saw blade in 1837. Farmers throughout the North American west bought his plow, called the "self-polisher." Since that time the John Deere Company and others have invented more and more equipment to help farmers. By 1910, motorized tractors had come into use on large farms. More food could be produced, using less people to do it.

Today, mechanical tractors are used in nearly every part of farm work, including planting, plowing, and harvesting.

This illustration shows the Aztec people building Chinampas, or floating fields.

The innovative Aztec

The Aztecs settled in Tenochtitlan, present-day Mexico City, in the 1100s and were surrounded by strong, well-established neighbors. The Aztecs had to make use of swampy land for their farms. In order to prevent floods from drowning their crops, the Aztecs made stepped or terraced fields so that the excess water would run off. They also created barges, called Chinampas. These artificial islands were made out of woven reeds and covered with mud. The Chinampas were anchored to the swamp floor with plant roots and used as a "floating field" where Aztec farmers grew their crops, including corn, squash, peppers, beans, and tomatoes.

Irrigation

Irrigation is used to bring water to areas that do not naturally have water, and to take excess water away. Irrigation brings water to crops that need it to grow and thrive. If too much water is left on an irrigated field it becomes waterlogged, making it hard for plants to survive. Irrigation is as old as farming. From as far back as 6000 B.C., farmers created human-made lakes and canals to transport water to otherwise dry, unproductive lands.

Flood irrigation

The four main types of irrigation are flood, row, aerial, and drip. Flood irrigation is used to provide water to crops such as alfalfa, and to grains such as wheat, barley, and oats. It is also used in apple orchards and to grow rice crops. Water is spread all over the ground, and leaches through the soil. This form of irrigation works best on flat ground so that water does not run off and cause soil erosion.

(above) These workers are digging furrows for an irrigation system in the African country of Sudan.

(left) The simplest form of irrigation is using buckets to carry water from a water source and dumping it on crops.

Row irrigation

Row irrigation is mainly used for vegetables that are planted in furrows such as beets, onions, and carrots. Furrows, or rows, are dug alongside rows of plants. The furrows are filled with water, which soaks into the soil to feed the plants.

Aerial irrigation

Aerial irrigation is water applied to crops from overhead. This is done with powerful sprinkler systems that shoot water into the sky so that it falls down the same way rain does. This method of irrigation is often used for crops like corn and wheat. As it sprays, some of the water may **evaporate** before it lands on the crops or soaks into the soil.

(above) In drip irrigation, pipes carrying water are laid in fields.

Drip irrigation

Drip irrigation is a very efficient way of applying water to soil. Water trickles directly into the soil, so water is not lost due to evaporation or run-off. The water is also targeted to the exact spot it is needed. For these reasons drip irrigation is used in drier regions of North America.

(left) This rolling sprinkler is a type of aerial irrigation. The sprinklers are moved to different parts of the fields as needed.

Soil scientists

Soil scientists, or pedologists, study soil as a natural resource. Natural resources are things such as trees, water, minerals, and soil, that occur naturally and are used by people.

Scientists at work

Pedologists are interested in knowing how soil forms, what types of soil exist, and where they exist. Soil scientists are concerned with the use of soil by farmers, as well as how soil affects our environment. Sometimes soil scientists work with the people who plan new buildings in cities. They tell them whether or not the soil would make a good, stable spot to build. They also tell them if the soil is unique or important to our environment. Sometimes special or unique natural areas must be protected from development. When soil is polluted, soil scientists tell how bad the pollution is. They also suggest ways that might help clean the soil.

Testing the soil

Soil scientists test small samples of soil to find out if the nutrients that plants need to survive are in the soil. If scientists determine that the soil is missing certain nutrients, they determine what kind of fertilizer to apply to improve the soil quality. Soil scientists also test samples to measure the pH level of soil. A pH test tells a scientist how **acidic** the soil is. If the acid level is too high, **limestone** dust can be applied to reduce the acidity. By testing the soil rather than guessing, farmers can ensure that they apply the right sort of nutrients to help maintain a balanced soil.

Soil scientists test new ways to irrigate and measure how much moisture is in the soil .

Getting dirty is part of a soil scientist's job! Feeling the soil is one of the best ways to test it.

Baking dirt

Scientists can also test how dense soil is, how much water it will need, and the size of the individual particles. To test the moisture content of soil, scientists bake it in an oven! First, they measure the weight of the soil sample. Then the soil sample is baked at a very high temperature. This causes any water that was stored in the soil to evaporate. The scientist then weighs the soil again. The soil weighs less than it did before it was baked. The difference in weight tells the scientist how much moisture was stored in the original soil sample.

What is in that soil?

One way scientists test soil to see what types of particles it contains is to put a sample in a beaker and add water. The largest and heaviest particles sink to the bottom and the smallest and lightest remain on top. In the soil sample below, the sand particles sunk to the bottom. Above the sand is silt, followed by clay particles.

Uses of sand & soil

Soil not only supplies people with a place to grow their food; it also helps keep our ground water supply clean. As rain water leaches through the soil it takes pollutants with it. Before leaching into the ground water, many of these pollutants are trapped by soil. In this way, soil acts as a filter, keeping unwanted elements from entering our water supply.

Foundations

Soil creates a solid foundation on which people build structures, such as homes and schools. Sometimes, new neighborhoods are constructed on sites that have good soil for farming. Soil is so important to life that some communities are now beginning to protect valuable farmland by only allowing houses to be built on sites where the soil is not the best soil available for farming.

Homes of mud

In some parts of the world, buildings and houses are made from mud bricks. Soil is mixed with water, and other materials such as straw, and shaped into bricks. When the bricks harden, they become strong blocks used to create homes.

These beehive-shaped homes were built of mud bricks in Turkey.

Making glass

Sand and soil are also used in manufacturing. Glass is made by fusing sand with other ingredients, including potash and soda. These ingredients are heated to a very high temperature until they are liquid. The mixture is poured into one large sheet on top of a layer of molten metal. The glass stays there until it hardens. The glass solidifies without being touched by other materials, and the final product has a perfectly smooth finish.

Concrete

Gravel is large particles of rock. Gravel is mixed with cement. Cement is a gray powder created from crushed limestone. When gravel and cement are mixed together they form concrete, a common material used to make roads, sidewalks, and buildings.

(above) To shape glass into bottles, air is blown through a tube into the liquid mixture.

(below) A gravel quarry where gravel is crushed.

Erosion

People cannot create new soil. It is a non-renewable resource. Every second, about 10,000 acres (4,050 hectares) of healthy soil are lost because of erosion. Erosion occurs when rain or wind carries soil away.

Wind and water

Wind erosion happens when wind blows over fields and picks up soil particles and carries them off. Much of this soil is deposited into the seas. Water also causes erosion. As rain falls and flows across the land it carries soil with it, washing it away into rivers and streams.

The right side of this picture shows a forest that has been clear-cut. In clear-cutting, all the trees are cut down. On slopes, the loss of roots to hold the soil in place leads to erosion.

Erosion by human factors

Erosion can also be caused by human influence. When land is **clear-cut**, the soil becomes vulnerable. With no root systems to anchor it down, the soil loosens, and can more easily be swept or washed away. Overgrazing is another cause of erosion. Many animals, including goats, sheep, llamas, and cattle, graze on fields of grass. Grasslands play an important role in keeping the soil in place. When grazing animals are permitted to overeat in one area, the loss of plants threatens the soil. Erosion often leads to **desertification** in these areas.

Protecting against erosion

Plants are the soil's best defense against erosion. Root systems help anchor the soil down, while leaves and stalks protect the soil from wind and rain. Larger plants help reduce the impact of wind. Often a row of trees is planted along the outside of a farmer's field, creating a barrier against wind erosion. Much has been learned about erosion, and farmers now have new practices that help preserve their valuable topsoil.

Terraces

Erosion is common on hillsides where **gravity** works with rainwater to wash soil downhill. Some farmers create levels or terraces in their fields. These series of flat levels, much like a staircase, reduce the steepness of hills, and help keep the topsoil from washing away.

Contour plowing

Like terracing, contour plowing works to reduce the impact of gravity on the soil, especially on hills. Plows leave long ruts in the soil. Water naturally streams into the ruts. If the ruts run downhill, the water will run off, taking the soil with it. By plowing along lines that are at right angles to the slope of the land surface, or contour plowing, the water does not run off as quickly, and more soil stays safely in place.

Trees are planted around these kiwi fruit orchards to protect them from the wind.

No tillage plowing

Tilling is a farming practice that leaves soil bare for several months of the year. Tilling removes plants that cover the soil. When farmers till, their plows reach into the A and B horizons of the soil, tearing up the roots of plants. The lack of coverage and the destruction of roots leave the soil loose, and vulnerable to erosion. When farmers practice no tillage plowing, they take only the fruits or vegetables from their crops, and leave the stalks and roots in place. This also leaves seeds on the ground, which take root for the next harvest.

Protecting the soil

It is important to protect our soil from erosion and pollution. New soil takes many years to form, and it is being lost at a faster rate than it is being created. Almost one-fifth of the land surface of the earth has suffered soil damage from overgrazing, clear-cutting, and poor land use.

Fertilizing

Over time, soils can become depleted of their nutrients. Plants remove the nutrients from the soil, which are not replaced as quickly as they are used. Nutrients can be replaced in the soil by adding fertilizer. Some fertilizers are human-made, while others are natural. In many places human waste is made into a fertilizer called sludge.

Sludge is very rich in nutrients, and is applied to farmers' fields. All fertilizers, natural or man-made, can be dangerous. In addition to their nutrients they contain **nitrates** and bacteria that can be dangerous to people. Sometimes rainfall can cause these fertilizers to leach into drinking wells. When people drink the water, they become extremely ill.

Cleaning the soil

Soil can be damaged by pollution. Chemicals can leach into the soil, either through dumping or accidental spills. When soil is polluted it must be cleaned to remove the chemicals that are dangerous to humans and the organisms that help keep the soil healthy. Some plants draw pollutants out of soil. Soils that have been contaminated by heavy metals can be cleaned with bulrushes. These plants, also known as cattails, draw the chemicals out of the soil up through their roots. This moves the contaminants from the soil and into the plant.

Killing pests

Things we do to protect our plants can hurt the soil. People sometimes apply chemicals to crops, flowers, and grass. Herbicides are chemicals that kill unwanted weeds that compete with other plants for nutrients. Pesticides are chemicals that kill bugs. These chemicals help eliminate weeds and bugs, but they poison the soil, hurt or kill the many organisms that live in the soil, and make it unhealthy.

Soil compaction

When farm equipment is used too often and crops are repeatedly planted without allowing the soil to rest, the result is compaction of the soil. The soil is depleted of its nutrients, and does not have the valuable air pockets it needs for water to travel through it. The soil is no longer an ideal place for animals to live, and it loses productivity.

Salinization

When irrigation is not properly managed, soil becomes waterlogged, or salinization occurs. Salinization is when the salt levels in soil begin to build up. Eventually there is so much salt in the soil that it becomes poisonous for plants and some soil-dwelling animals.

Enough food?

If we continue to damage the soil, there may not be enough healthy soil to produce all the food needed to feed the people of the world. Farmers and scientists are working together to find ways to conserve soil so that our supply is better protected.

(top) These Ethiopians are waiting for food to be distributed. Drought caused crops to fail and millions of people in this African country were left without food.

Glossary

acidic The measure of how much acid something has. Acid is a bitter chemical

bacteria Tiny, single-celled organisms

castings An earthworm's waste

clear-cutting Cutting down all the trees in an area at the same time, leaving the land bare

compact Having parts that are closely packed together

contract To pull together and make smaller

decomposed Rotted, or broken down

desertification To change arable land into a desert through poor land practice

erosion A process by which something is worn away, bit by bit

evaporate To change from a liquid into a gas

expand To pull apart and get larger

fertile Land that is good for growing crops

fertilizer A substance added to soil that contains plant nutrients

food web Two or more food chains that connect when a member of one food chain eats a member of another food chain

glaciers Large, slowly moving sheets of ice

gravity The force that surrounds bodies in space

inorganic Not living

irrigate To supply water to crops

leaches To slowly drain through something

lichen A plant made up of a fungus and algae growing together

life cycle The birth, life, and death of a plant or animal

limestone A type of rock sometimes made from corals or shells.

minerals Non-living, naturally occurring substances

nitrate A type of chemical that plants need for growth

nitrogen A colorless, odorless gas

nutrients Something that nourishes, or provides food necessary for good health

organic Living organisms

organisms A living thing, such as a plant or animal

parasites Animals that live off other animals

photosynthesis The process by which plants take sunlight, water, and carbon dioxide and turn them into food

pollutants Something that pollutes, or makes dirty

single-celled Being made up only one kind of cell. All living things are made up of cells

Index

1 2 3 4 5 6 7 8 9 0   Printed in the U.S.A.   3 2 1 0 9 8 7 6 5 4